RHYTHMS *of a* FAITHFUL J:URNEY

Verses from Slavery to Presidency

ROBIN JOYCE MILLER ✋ JAMES WALTER MILLER

ARTWORK BY ROBIN JOYCE MILLER

The artwork for each quilt is mixed media collage. They all include decorative paper and fabric paint. Some works include acrylic and watercolor, as well.

ISBN: 1481134221

ISBN 13: 9781481134224

Library of Congress Control Number: 2012922913

CreatSpace Independent Publishing Platform

North Charleston, South Carolina

DEDICATION

To my mother, who was the first person to teach me about

faith through her stories and day-to-day living.

Robin

To Jason,

Keep the torch of faith and cultural pride burning in your spirit.

Much love,

Mom and Dad

ACKNOWLEDGEMENTS

Special thanks to Rev. Dr. Henry T. Simmons and the St. Albans Congregational Church for your continuing spiritual guidance and opportunities to develop our faith. We are humbled and most grateful.

The walls of the African American Museum of Hempstead, NY have been a home for my art and poetry for over a year. I would like to express my gratitude to David Byer-Tyre who introduced my history collection. And, of course, I could not forget Joysetta Pearse who continues to support my work, while encouraging and inspiring new ideas.

TABLE OF CONTENTS

INTRODUCTION

In 1999, I created my first mixed media collage quilt—*The Jazz History Quilt*. I enjoyed researching the information necessary for the narrative and planning the composition. Once this initial work was complete, I became passionate about creating more quilts with African American history themes. It was a wonderful way to study a subject, while developing an enormous sense of cultural pride. I pursued each project like someone amassing a valuable collection.

Writing poetry is something that my husband, Jim, and I have done for years. Traveling to Ghana with our church on a global exposure ministry trip in the summer of 2010 provided a new inspiration each day. The experiences of visiting Elmina and Cape Coast Castles, found on Ghana's coastline, were deeply moving. With heavy hearts, we began writing poems about slavery.

The following year the African American Museum of Nassau County (Hempstead, New York) requested that I exhibit my collection of mixed media collage quilts, entitled *Restoring My African Soul—An African American Journey*. A few of the quilts had accompanying poems. Later, we decided to create a poem for each quilt.

Sometimes the images served as the inspiration, but usually the inspirations came from our experiences growing up in a Christian African American environment. Faith in God flows throughout many of the verses. In an effort to feel more closely connected to our ancestors while creating the art, I frequently listened to Alvin Ailey American Dance Theater's CD, *Revelations*. This collection of Negro spirituals is the theme music of a people triumphing over adversity. Anyone who is familiar with "I've Been 'Buked" can easily see how those lyrics influenced the poem "Headin' North." Jim's six trips with our church to New Orleans to restore homes devastated by Katrina inspired a love for the beauty that still exists there.

We hope that this collection of narrative quilts and poetry speaks to the faith and fortitude of a people who refused to let their oppressive circumstances claim their destiny.

Robin

FAITH

Robin J. Miller

Faith
Unseen, but true
Stronger than any shackle
Stronger than any chain
Breaking through
To a new reality—
God's grace

FROM CAPTURE TO CHATT-HELL

James W. Miller

My ancestors' culture and way of life, stolen
From a homeland they may never again see
To take a journey from capture to Chatt-Hell*
The "dehumanizing process" called slavery.

At first kidnapped, disrespected, and tortured
Then shackled around the neck, hands, and feet
Deprived of space, slumber, nutrition, and water
To destroy the will, surrender—mission complete.

* Chatt-Hell – a play on the word chattel (slave)

JOURNEY TO HELL QUILT

Door of No Return

James W. Miller

Am I really here this morning?
Hearing drum's song the very last time

My identity and family are stolen
In chains I leave this country of mine

A slave object—no longer a person
Sold at auction and no longer free

The sailors and ships are arriving
My Lord, what will become my destiny?

Slave Castle Quilt

MIDDLE PASSAGE CARGO

Robin J. Miller

Knowing your struggle
Feeling your pain
Knowing from whence you came
Gives me faith in God up above
Gives me truths I can claim.

Knowing they tried to peel off your pride
With hatred, with bondage
Insane
But watching you rise
Above malice and lies
Gives me strength to walk proud without shame.

Knowing your faith and your fortitude
Knowing that I come from you
Gives me great courage
And I understand
There's nothing that I cannot do.

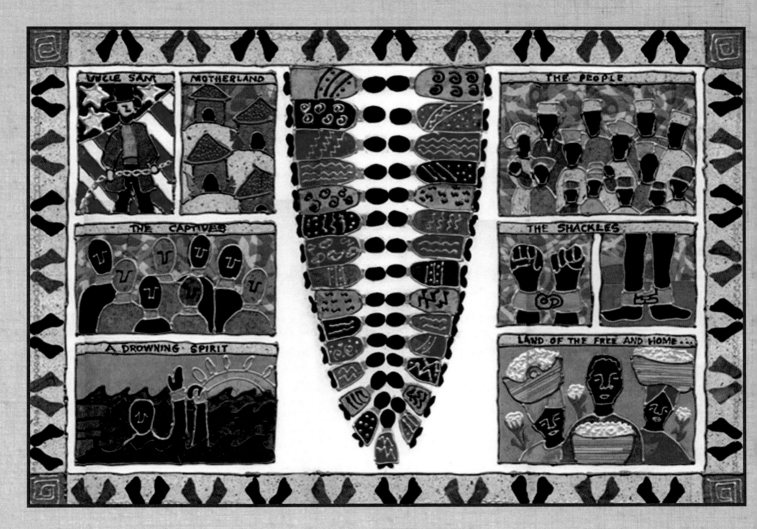

MIDDLE PASSAGE QUILT

RESTORING MY AFRICAN SOUL

James W. Miller

Kidnapped, separated from
My ancestral motherland
Shackled, chained, displayed
Subservient to humanity

Umbilical cord to my
African Soul—broken
Slave for a price
Boats pulled out to sea

On the other side of prayer and faith
Lie the heavens and divinity
Shackles and chains removed
A majestic hand ended slavery

Still, world forces test
The strength of my feeding bowl
To conquer the battle for victory
I call on God to
Restore my African soul

ANOTHER COTTON PICKIN' DAY

THE PLANTATION

Robin J. Miller

Born to a world where white is pure
Where black is soot and dirt
Yet you work with dignity, with pride, with grace
Though your heart is heavy with hurt.

Born to a world where white is pure
Where blackness has little worth
But God plants his seeds in dirt called soil,
A soil that nurtures and feeds the earth.

Born to a world where white is pure
Where you struggle just to survive
Know that your harvest is near
Toil in faith, have no fear
Soon you will flourish and thrive.

PLANTATION QUILT

ESCAPE

James W. Miller

Hush now, be alert
Use your eyes to see
Grab your hobo bags
Then come and follow me

Out behind the stables
Under a barbwire fence
Through the tall cornfields
Endless and ever dense

Keep movin' forward
Never look back
In the distance, gunfire…
Barks of a hound dog pack

Through rain, scorching sun
Under the moonlight glow
Rooms in hidden places
Of folks we do not know

How we pray all night,
Every second of the day
For faith's shield to provide
Protection along the way

Praise the Lord Almighty!
Escaped from masta's hand
Climbing to the mountaintop
Into freedom's land

Underground Railroad Legend Quilt

JUNETEENTH

Robin J. Miller

Heard some talk of freedom
In the Texas wind
Spoken in soft whispers
Time and time again.

Then a major general
Spoke loud and crystal clear
"Emancipation Proclamation"
Mercy—finally here!

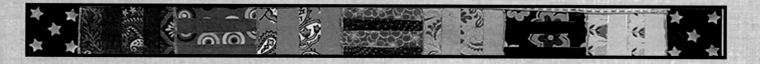

JUNETEENTH HISTORY QUILT

HEADIN' NORTH

Robin J. Miller

Been so 'buked
Been so scorned
Headin' north sho's I's born.

Ain't no jobs
Ain't nothing fair
Boll weevils
Floods are everywhere.

Want no part
No Jim, No Crow
Can't pick no cotton
Not no mo'.

Seen some folks a hangin'
Got me lookin' in the skies
Where you at, Lord Jesus?
Can't you hear our mournful cries?

Gotta get me a ticket
Gotta get us on a train
Get my family to somewhere,
Somewhere that be sane.

Been so 'buked
Been so scorned
Headin' north sho's I's born.

GREAT MIGRATION QUILT

Renaissance

James W. Miller

1920s Harlem created a flame
The world would see.
1920s Harlem changed the fabric
Of American history.

It had its own intelligence
It had its own rules and rights
It had its own expression
It had its own electric nights.

It had its own community
It had its own power

It had its own police
It's own food twenty-four hour.

It had its own swagger
It had its own beat
It had its own entertainment
It had its own musical street.

It had its own rhythm
It had its own smile
It had its own culture
It had its own style.

Harlem.

HARLEM RENAISSANCE QUILT

Jazz Is

Robin J. Miller

What is jazz?

Jazz is shakin' and strummin'
It's ticklin' and drummin'
Jazz is tappin' and singin'
Real smooth.

It's playin' while struttin'
It's fingerin' and plucklin'
And jazz has a history, too.

Jazz is rompin' and stompin'
It's mad finger poppin'
It's hot, yet it's so very cool.

Jazz can be three musicians
Playin' trio style
Or a duet that has only two.

Jazz can moan and groan
On the saxophone
'Cause somebody's playin' the blues.

But my kind of jazz is best of all
It's sittin' and listenin'
And feelin' the vibes
With a jazzy attitude.

That's jazzzzzzzzzzzzzz!!

JAZZ HISTORY QUILT

Robin Joyce Miller / James Walter Miller   23

Where Are the People Who Care?

Robin J. Miller

Where are the people who care?
Where are the people who long to march
Who long to walk
Who long to run in the greatest race,
The *human race?*
I *know* that these people are there!

Where are the people who hear the cry
For peace and harmony
And want to be part of something
Much greater than hate?
I *know* that these people are there!

Where are the people who dreamed the dream
And walked with King, both *black* and *white*
The people who fought the *nonviolent fight?*
I *know* that these people are there!

Where are the people who look at a face
And see not a color, not religion, nor race
But look into the heart and the soul of someone
And make their judgment that way?
I *know* that these people are there!

Where are the people who claim to love God
Who claim to love man
And not merely façade
Who claim to be brothers and sisters on Earth?
I *know* that these people are there!

Though these people are there
And we know that you care
We don't hear your soft voices
Ringing loud! Ringing clear!
Please speak up! Show yourselves!
Please come out from your shells
And tell *all* the world that you care!

CIVIL RIGHTS MOVEMENT QUILT

Robin Joyce Miller / JamesWalter Miller   25

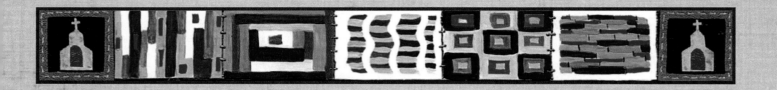

THE SPIRIT OF GEE'S BEND

Robin J. Miller

God is in our music
Hear our spirits grow
We lift our voices to Him
His help is all we know.

God is in our very hands
He guides each stitch we sew
We stretch our hands unto the Lord
Or whither would we go?

GEE'S BEND QUILT

March on, Brothers

Robin J. Miller

We keep the rhythm
We move our feet
March on, brothers
Keep that beat!

Moving together
Walking so tall
No pants hanging down
No way, not at all.

Too proud to allow
Our butts to hang out
That's *not* the movement,
Not what we're about.

Marching to take our
Communities back
Proving to all

Men with pride
Can be black.

Can't sit around
Watching homelessness, drugs
No patience for violence,
Illiteracy, and thugs.

Can't have our children
In fatherless homes
Children unsupervised,
Unloved, and alone.

We must keep the rhythm
We must move our feet
We must march on, brothers
We must keep that beat!

MILLION MAN MARCH QUILT

Robin Joyce Miller / James Walter Miller   29

Big Easy
James W. Miller

The walk and the talk are not magnified
The Big Easy's like an old pair of jeans
The architecture and form arrest your eyes
The culture, romance, the jazz of New Orleans

Where stories are told at the drop of a hat
Where overgrown trees shade you from the endless sky
Where cars, trucks, bikes, electric trolley cars
Landscaped streets of people parading by

Oh the sights, sounds, flavors of Cajun cooking
What better place to experience new delights?
Oh how easy to fall in love with New Orleans
The city's charms enchant—
All mornings, all noons, all nights

New Orleans Quilt

THE JOURNEY

James W. Miller

Once treated as objects of service
With some remote human quality
American economy flourished
From the institution of slavery

Battles made laws change over time
Emancipation
Reconstruction
Integration
Civil rights
Right to vote
Leadership
Gave us a voice to address the nation

Recognize the fabric of sacrifice
God's required journey fee
God's grace transformed us
From picking cotton…to presidency.

JOURNEY QUILT

INAUGURATION DAY 2009

Robin J. Miller

O-BA-MA! O-BA-MA!
A day to scream and shout
O-BA-MA! O-BA-MA!
Massive crowds came out.

The trumpets bellowed loudly
The bells rang through the air
Pomp and circumstance were felt
Just magic—*everywhere*!

People waved their flags about
The red, the white, the blue
Echoes of a dream once heard
Sweet victory come true.

Prayers were lifted
Speeches made
Aretha came to sing

From every mountainside we know
Let peace and freedom ring.

My country, 'tis of thee
Sweet land of liberty
Of thee I sing.

Obama's oath was taken
"Hail to the Chief" was played
The cannons fired through the air
Out rolled his motorcade.

They cruised past waving people
You heard more screams and shouts
God bless our first black family
En route to the "White" House.

Glory! Hallelujah!
I heard our forefathers sing—
"From every mountainside we know
Let peace and freedom ring!"

INAUGURATION DAY QUILT

Made in the USA
San Bernardino, CA
29 May 2016